Princess Penelope (Mulan),
Walk in Love!
~Lydia

God's Princess Forever
Discover Your Royal Identity & Reach Your True Potential

Written and Illustrated by

Lydia Joy, MBA

Text and Illustrations Copyright © 2016 by Lydia Joy, MBA

God's Princess Forever
Discover Your Royal Identity & Reach Your True Potential
by Lydia Joy, MBA

Printed in the United States of America.

Edited by Xulon Press.

ISBN 9781498461580

All rights reserved solely by the author. The author guarantees all contents are original and do not infringe upon the legal rights of any other person or work. No part of this book may be reproduced in any form without the permission of the author. The views expressed in this book are not necessarily those of the publisher.

Unless otherwise indicated, Scripture taken from the Holy Bible, Today's New International Version™ TNIV ® Copyright © 2001, 2005 by International Bible Society ®. All rights reserved worldwide.

www.xulonpress.com

Presented to God's Princess Forever:

_____

By:

_____

On:

_____

"See that you do not despise one of these little ones. For I tell you that their angels in heaven always see the face of my Father in heaven."
  Matthew 18:10-11

"For this God is our God forever and ever;
He will be our guide even to the end."

Psalm 48:14

Gracey, a young girl, enjoyed reading storybooks. She read about all the well-known princesses when she discovered a similar pattern in the fairy tales. Gracey noticed that every princess had a prince who rescued her from difficult situations, and in the end they lived happily ever after. Cinderella had a prince, the mermaid had her prince and, in every other fairy tale, there seemed to be a sleeping princess who woke up to the kiss of her prince. Then, Gracey started wondering, "Who will be my prince that will come to my rescue when I need help?"

Thinking about it further, Gracey longed for a prince to come to her rescue when she encountered trouble at school. Andy, a troublemaker in her class, was annoyed that Gracey could run faster than him. He would do everything in his power to pick on her. At times, when Gracey would wear her hair in pigtails, Andy would pull the bows out of her hair.

When her friend Luke noticed the trouble Andy was causing Gracey, he came to help her. At that point, Gracey started to imagine that Luke might be her prince and knight in shining armor, who would come to her rescue all the time. However, Luke was completely unaware of the fairy-tale expectations she had of him.

Gracey quickly became disappointed because Luke wasn't always around to come rescue her. On her own, Gracey would do her best to avoid Andy or run away from him. Other times, she would try to get back at him by reminding him that he couldn't run as fast as her, which would annoy Andy even more.

Upset about the situation, Gracey decided to tell her dad about what she was dealing with at school. She described to him how, in the fairy tales, every princess had a prince who came to her rescue when in trouble. Gracey explained how she thought that her friend Luke might be her rescuing prince, only to later realize that he really didn't meet her expectations. With frustration in her voice, she asked, "How come I don't have a prince who will always come to my rescue when I need help?"

This question got the attention of her mom, who was nearby preparing dinner for the family. Her dad cleared his throat as he responded, "Gracey, sweetheart, you may not have the type of prince you read about in fairy tales, but you actually have the greatest prince of all, the Prince of Peace, your Savior and God's son, Jesus, who came on this earth to save you, so that you could be a part of an eternal kingdom. It's important that you understand your royal identity and whose princess you actually are."

"The everlasting King of the universe and our Heavenly Father, God, who gave you as a gift to your mother and I, first and foremost; that's who you belong to. As God's children, we are all His princes and princesses. In the eyes of God, you are His princess forever, and He loves you more than anyone could ever love you. His amazing love is unconditional, and He will always be there for you, no matter what situation you may be facing. In His instruction manual to us, the Holy Bible, it is written, 'For this God is our God forever and ever; He will be our guide even to the end.' (Psalm 48:14) This true God, who we trust and believe, made many other promises of blessing in His Word that are applicable to us today."

"As God's princess, you also have a guardian angel who watches over you all the time. In this life, you will encounter happiness as well as challenges; but God will give you wisdom in how to handle them."

"In addition, when you look in the mirror, you have to believe that God is your wonderful Creator and see yourself as He sees you, for you are His masterpiece. You are uniquely beautiful and were wonderfully created in God's image. Believing all this should help you be confident in who God created you to be, for He is the true source of your confidence."

"If you long to have a prince that you could marry someday, just like I'm your mom's prince, you will someday meet him; but you have to pray and trust God to write your own love story."

"Concerning Andy at school, know that God and your guardian angel are protecting you, even in those circumstances. However, you still have to respectfully stand up to Andy for yourself, instead of expecting your friend Luke to do something every time. In certain situations, people who have been hurt by others end up mistreating other people, and they need our kindness the most. God blessed each of us with great strengths and talents, including Andy; although his talents may be different than yours," her dad concluded.

By this time, dinner was ready, and as they shared the meal together, Gracey curiously asked, "But what are my strengths and talents?" Her mom lovingly replied, "Your dad and I will help you recognize them through a fun activity that will help you see your true potential."

Starting with Gracey, they created a "Talents and Faith Visions" board for each member of their family. On the front of the board, they answered valuable questions about each other to uncover their talents and what they appreciated or admired in one another. They also made suggestions for any areas in need of improvement.

On the back of the board, they made their dreams come to life by creating a unique visual of their goals, so they can fulfill their God-given purposes. They had the philosophy that if they have faith for anything within God's will, and do their part in achieving it, God will take care of the rest.

As a result of doing this activity, Gracey became more confident as she learned, from her loving parents, some of the qualities and talents they recognized in her.

She planned to look at the board daily and prayed that God would lead her every step in the right direction to accomplish her true purpose. That night, when Gracey went to bed, she had a dream.

Gracey saw the most heavenly scenery and a majestic castle. Then a beautiful angel appeared, saying, "Gracey, I am Gabriella, your guardian angel, and I was assigned to you by your precious Creator, God, to watch over you all the days of your life."

"Just like a great tree is known by the quality of its fruits, as God's princess forever, distinguish yourself by always striving to produce these types of fruits in your life: starting with love and kindness; followed by joy, peace, patience, goodness, faithfulness, gentleness and self-control. (Galatians 5:22-23) You will reap the reward of many blessings, as a result of exemplifying such valuable qualities in your life."

When Gracey woke up that morning, she was inspired to do an act of love and kindness towards Andy. She wrote a note to Andy, explaining that God created each person with unique abilities; and that it wasn't right when she compared her running abilities to his, because he was gifted in other areas. Gracey also complimented Andy on the strengths and talents she admired in him. To accompany the note, she gave him an apple, his favorite snack.

Surprised and touched by Gracey's unexpected kind actions, Andy apologized for his own mistakes. He described how his older brothers constantly picked on him, so he thought it was okay to pick on others. As a result of Gracey's kind and loving act, Andy decided to start treating others the way that he would want to be treated. He realized that there were better solutions in dealing with conflict.

Surprisingly, Andy and Gracey became friends; together, they came up with different ways to show love and kindness to others. In the end, by discovering her royal identity, Gracey learned to depend on God, who will always be there for her instead of her friend Luke, who had the best of intentions. As God's princess forever, Gracey trusted the eternal King to be the author of her life story, which is destined to be better than any fairy tale.

Happily
Ever
After becomes a
Victorious reality to those who love God, the
Eternal King, and accept His gift of salvation; for their
Names are written in the Book of Life.

My Dear Princess _____

I love you so much that I gave my one and only Son so that if you believe in Him, you will not perish but have eternal life. *John 3:16*
I knew you before I formed you in your mother's womb. Before you were born I set you apart. *Jeremiah 1:5*
I know the plans I have for you… plans to prosper you and not to harm you, plans to give you hope and a future. *Jeremiah 29:11*
You will be a crown of splendor and a royal diadem in my hand. *Isaiah 62:3*
My kingdom is an everlasting kingdom, and my dominion endures through all generations. *Psalm 145:13*
Grace, mercy and peace from me, your Father and from Jesus Christ, my Son will be with you in truth and love. *2 John 1:3* Blessed are you, who persevere under trial, because when you have stood the test, you will receive the crown of life that I, God have promised to those who love me. *James 1:12*
Call to me and I will answer you and tell you great and unsearchable things you do not know. *Jeremiah 33:3*
I am able to do immeasurably more for you than all you ask or imagine… *Ephesians 3:20*
Delight in me and I will give you the desires of your heart. *Psalm 37:4*
You can do everything though me, your God who gives you strength. *Philippians 4:13* I go before you and will be with you, I will never leave you nor forsake you. Do not be afraid; do not be discouraged. *Deuteronomy 31:8*
For I will be your God forever and ever; I will be your guide even to the end. *Psalm 48:14*

Love Always, Your Heavenly Father and Everlasting King,

God

P.S. For I will command my angels concerning you to guard you in all your ways. *Psalm 91:11*
(Some scriptures have been paraphrased to reflect God speaking directly to you)

Check or write the talents, strengths and gifts that God has blessed you with:

- ☆ Loving
- ☆ Kind
- ☆ Joyful
- ☆ Gentle
- ☆ Faithful
- ☆ Patient
- ☆ Peaceful
- ☆ Diligent
- ☆ Artistic
- ☆ Athletic
- ☆ Creative
- ☆ Friendly
- ☆ Generous
- ☆ Optimistic
- ☆ Respectful
- ☆ Empathetic
- ☆ Smart/Wise
- ☆ Encourager
- ☆ Considerate
- ☆ Courageous
- ☆ Great leader
- ☆ Responsible
- ☆ Disciplined
- ☆ Trustworthy

- ☆ Good-natured
- ☆ Self-controlled
- ☆ Positive attitude
- ☆ Great listener
- ☆ Gifted singer
- ☆ Effective reader
- ☆ Great speaker
- ☆ Talented writer
- ☆ Inspiring storyteller
- ☆ Good at memorization
- ☆ Great sense of humor
- ☆ Intriguing personality
- ☆ Ability to handle change
- ☆ Speak a foreign language
- ☆ Effective at resolving conflict
- ☆ Apologize quickly when wrong
- ☆ Play an instrument well _____
- ☆ Great at playing _____
- ☆ _____
- ☆ _____
- ☆ _____
- ☆ _____
- ☆ _____

True Royal Confidence Tips:

★ Believe that you are God's princess forever, and He will always be there for you.

★ Believe that you were placed on this earth for a great purpose, to fulfill your God-given destiny.

★ Believe that God is the source of your confidence. Think, listen, talk, envision and act as a princess, the daughter of an eternal King.

★ Believe that God loves you unconditionally, and He offers you eternal life in heaven.

★ Believe that God has a guardian angel watching over you.

★ Believe that God will always hear your prayers, and He enjoys talking to you.

★ Believe that you have been forgiven and your past doesn't define you or determine your future.

★ Believe that you can overcome any fears with your faith in God and His amazing promises to you.

True Royal Confidence Tips:

★ Believe that God always wants the best for you, and He left His instruction manual, the Holy Bible, to guide you in making the right decisions for your life.

★ Believe that you are equipped to be full of love, kindness, joy, peace, patience, goodness, faithfulness, gentleness and self-control.

★ Believe that you are uniquely beautiful and were wonderfully created in God's image. See yourself through God's eyes, for He considers you one of His masterpieces. Do your best to take care of the incredible body God blessed you with.

★ Believe what God says about you, not the negative/hurtful comments of others.

★ Believe that God has gifted you with unique abilities/talents to use and bless others with.

★ Believe that God has great plans for you. Pray and trust Him to write your life/love story.

★ Believe that God can help you accomplish the dreams and desires He placed in your heart.

★ Believe that with God, all things are possible, and depend on Him for everything.

Love & Kindness Challenge ☺

Discover how many acts of love and kindness you can complete.

- ♥ Smile ☺
- ♥ Tell your family/friends how wonderful they are and how happy you are to have them in your life.
- ♥ Spend quality time with loved ones, and then tell them what you enjoyed most about being in their company.
- ♥ Randomly write someone a note about what you appreciate about him/her.
- ♥ Give a hug to your loved ones.
- ♥ Say "I love you" with meaning.
- ♥ Offer a compliment about someone's accomplishments or appearance.
- ♥ Show genuine interest when someone is speaking and give him/her your undivided attention.
- ♥ Make eye contact when listening and speaking to someone.
- ♥ Listen to understand the feelings behind the words without interrupting.
- ♥ Speak in a kind voice when communicating with others.
- ♥ Be patient and remain calm in a disagreement. If things escalate to the point that you or someone else may say or do something that will end in regret, then walk away and agree to postpone the conversation.
- ♥ Ask "What can I do to help you?"
- ♥ Be quick to sincerely say "I'm sorry" when wrong.
- ♥ Be respectful and polite. Say "Please", "Thank you" and "Would you be so kind to..."
- ♥ Write a thank-you note acknowledging someone else's kindness to you.
- ♥ Make a note to remember someone's birthday and make or buy him/her a card or gift.
- ♥ Acknowledge/respect someone's feelings.
- ♥ Respect someone's wishes by considering what he/she wants.
- ♥ Welcome new kids to your neighborhood, school, church, etc.

Love & Kindness Challenge ☺ continued...
Discover how many acts of love and kindness you can complete.

- ♥ Invite other kids to play with you and include everyone.
- ♥ Share your toys when playing with others.
- ♥ Hold a door open for someone and let him/her go in first.
- ♥ Help someone with his/her daily task.
- ♥ Do a household chore without being asked.
- ♥ Bring someone his/her favorite snack or make his/her favorite food.
- ♥ Offer up your seat to someone who is standing.
- ♥ Don't wake up someone who wants to sleep.
- ♥ Make someone else's bed.
- ♥ See people through the eyes of God, by reminding them of who they are in Him and the wonderful plans He has in store for their life.
- ♥ Treat others the way that you would want to be treated.
- ♥ Use your words to uplift, edify and encourage others including yourself. Don't say hurtful comments or make fun of other people, but try to look for something you admire about them.
- ♥ Offer someone a drink of water.
- ♥ Draw a picture for someone.
- ♥ Give someone a flower.
- ♥ Donate the toys and clothes you're not using anymore.
- ♥ Visit a sick friend and write him/her an encouraging note.
- ♥ Express empathy when someone is hurting or going through a difficult time.
- ♥ Choose a book a friend might like and lend it to him/her.
- ♥ Write encouraging messages or notes and leave them in places where others could find them.
- ♥ Volunteer for a good cause.

Closing thoughts from the author…

I pray this book helped you discover your royal identity, including the true love and promises God has for you. I hope that it inspires you to show sincere love and kindness to others. It is my desire that you recognize the unique talents that you have been blessed with, and have true confidence in who God created you to be, so you can reach your full potential. Regardless of the situation, remember to always depend on God first because He wants the best for you. If you have not had the opportunity to invite God to be your everlasting King, I would be honored to be a part of your eternal crowning by asking you to sincerely pray this important prayer with me:

Dear God… Please come into my heart and be my everlasting King. I believe that you sent your Son, Jesus, to save me when He died for all my sins, so that I can enjoy your amazing gift of eternal life. Please forgive my sins and guide my every step, so that I honor you in all my thoughts, words and actions. I love you, and help me to follow you and depend on you for the rest of my life. I pray by faith in Jesus' name. Amen.

As a result of your decision, the angels in heaven are rejoicing and your name has been written in God's Book of Life. May our everlasting King bless your journey, while you reign as God's princess forever.

Love, your sister in God's kingdom,

Lydia

Please visit www.GodsPrincessForever.com for more motivational and encouraging resources.